# FACEBOOK
## SAFETY AND PRIVACY

**TRACY BROWN**

New York

Published in 2014 by The Rosen Publishing Group, Inc.
29 East 21st Street, New York, NY 10010

**Library of Congress Cataloging-in-Publication Data**

Brown, Tracy.
Facebook safety and privacy/Tracy Brown. — 1st ed. —
New York: Rosen, © 2014
         p. cm. — (21st century safety and privacy)
Includes bibliographical references and index.
ISBN: 978-1-4488-9569-4 (Library Binding)
ISBN: 978-1-4488-9580-9 (Paperback)
ISBN: 978-1-4488-9581-6 (6-pack)
1. Online social networks—Security measures. 2. Internet—
Safety measures—Juvenile literature. 3. Internet—Security measures—
Juvenile literature. 4. Facebook (Electronic resource)—Juvenile literature.
5. Privacy, Right of—Juvenile literature. I. Title.
HM742 .B76 2014
006.754'083

*Manufactured in the United States of America*

CPSIA Compliance Information: Batch #S13YA: For further information, contact Rosen Publishing, New York, New York, at 1-800-237-9932.

# CONTENTS

# INTRODUCTION

Facebook CEO Mark Zuckerberg smiles while making a speech at a technology conference in San Francisco, California, on September 11, 2012.

**M**ark Zuckerberg was studying psychology and computer science when he created the first version of what became Facebook. It was the perfect product of his interest in human nature and technology and his mission to make the world a more open place. He understood that people like to connect and share information, and he had the computer skills to help them do it.

Facebook is now used by more than nine hundred million people around the world. It is a platform where people can connect for the first time or reconnect with others from their past. The downside is that sometimes we share too much information with too many people and put ourselves at risk.

How can you enjoy the power of Facebook while maintaining an appropriate level of privacy? Read on to find ways to control your content and who can view it so that your Facebook experience stays fun, secure, and safe.

# CHAPTER ONE

# KEEPING A LOW PROFILE

**F**acebook gives its users a tool that allows them to share and connect with others. With Facebook, every member has his or her own individual space to post links to interesting sites or online articles, personal photographs and videos, and daily status updates, among other things.

The space, referred to as a wall or timeline, also allows users to provide personal details about themselves. You can share anything from your hometown to your favorite food or your birth date to what school you attend.

You can post notes, share scores from games, tell people what music you are listening to, and let everyone know which parties you plan to attend. You can share what products and music and movies are your favorites and join and organize groups and events.

Facebook is a remarkable tool for social interaction and businesses alike. However, there is also a potential downside to Facebook. The more you share on your timeline, the more everyone out there on the Internet knows about you. You have to be very cautious about controlling your own content on Facebook in order to protect yourself and your privacy in the real world.

Mark Zuckerberg unveils the timeline while delivering the keynote speech at the Facebook f8 conference on September 22, 2011. The timeline radically transformed the look and feel of Facebook.

From the privacy of your own bedroom or at school—wherever you get online—it is easy to forget just how many people can access the information on your Facebook timeline. Something as seemingly innocent as posting your address on your timeline can let the wrong people know where you are—people who want to take advantage of this information and use it for purposes you don't intend.

this information and use it for purposes you don't intend.

# What Not to Share

In an increasingly digitized, globalized world, in which anyone with a smart phone can access endless streams of information online, it is crucial that you understand the dangers of giving away too much information online. Not that you shouldn't use and enjoy Facebook and other sites, but you should think twice before sharing anything online.

Think about it: you exercise caution every day when you share information off-line. If you are going to tell a good friend a secret on the school bus, you talk in a quiet voice and look around to see if anyone who should not hear is listening. You probably don't want everyone to listen in on your private telephone calls. There are things in life you want some people to know but

The Facebook application for the iPhone is distributed by Apple and is one of the most popular social networking apps.

Just because Facebook allows you to share many details about yourself—phone number, e-mail address, and so on—that doesn't mean you have to overshare. You can opt to not provide any details other than your name. Don't feel pressure to provide more about yourself than you feel comfortable with.

Although Facebook provides many options for you to limit who has access to your timeline, you have more power than anyone over how much your content is shared and with whom. Simply put: the best way to maintain your privacy online is to not post in the first place. If you don't share something in the first place, you won't have a problem. Even if you delete something later, there's no telling how many people saw it when it was posted on the site, and there's no guarantee it will be deleted permanently from the Facebook server. When in doubt, leave it out.

That doesn't mean you can't reveal anything about yourself. Instead of giving your exact address, share what town you live in. Instead of writing messages on people's timelines for anyone to see, send a private message or use Facebook's chat feature.

Be equally aware of other people's feelings and possible outcomes for them. If you are tempted to post a status update but worry that a friend of yours will have her feelings hurt by it or someone could get into trouble at school or at home, then don't share it. Always weigh the consequences. It's better to be overly cautious than to do something you'll regret.

# Choose Your Friends Wisely

The desire to be accepted socially by your peers is a common feeling. We all want to have friends, and we all want to be a friend to other people. Part of the draw of Facebook is that it tells you exactly how many Facebook friends you have. It is easy to be pulled in and want to increase this number. If you hit ninety-five, then why not aim for one hundred? Your friends have five hundred or more friends, shouldn't you?

According to research into so-called Facebook addiction, part of what compels people to use Facebook is the desire to accumulate as many friends as possible, regardless of whether a user has met these friends in person or not.

Searching for friends can also be a lot of fun. The older you are, the more people you have known in your life. And not all of the people you have encountered go to your school or live on your street. Maybe you met some of them at summer camp. Maybe you met some of them on your winter vacation, or maybe they live next door to your cousin who lives across the country. It can be exciting to reconnect with people from your past on Facebook and to keep seeing your number of friends grow.

It can also be easy to fall into the trap of wanting to appear "in" with certain people. If there are particularly popular kids at your school whom you want to hang out with, or a person you really have a crush on, it can be flattering to add them or be added to their profiles as a friend.

## > GET THE PICTURE?

A picture is worth a thousand words—and can do as much damage. If you are going to include any content that specifically involves another person—including photos or videos—make sure you have the person's permission to do so. Other people may be more conservative than you about what they want to share online. Always ask friends before posting photos of them or before you tag photos. Don't be shy about untagging yourself from a photo if you do not want your name attached to it.

It is so easy to get carried away making "friends" on Facebook that it is common to forget a simple fact: the more people you "friend" on Facebook, the more people who have access to your timeline, and the more people who can tag you in posts and photos. For this reason, it really is worth stopping to think before you friend someone, whether you send the friend request or he or she does.

Don't become friends with anyone who you are not sure will respect you, online and off. If someone is mean to you in person, that person will be mean to you online. If someone is a good friend to you in person, then you can likely trust him or her to treat you well on Facebook, too.

Cyberbullying—the abuse of a person through online or telephone technology—is a very real problem in the

Cyberbullying is among the downsides of social networking sites such as Facebook. Be very mindful of whom you accept or request as a friend, and make sure they will respect you online and off.

United States. Reports of suicides following cyberbullying episodes have recently gotten worldwide attention. Protect yourself by opening up your timeline only to people who you know will not use it against you.

Equally, do not friend strangers. There are far too many cases of adults or kids pretending to be someone they are not and preying on young people. You do not want to be the victim of a stalker or anyone who could harm you. Make sure you know with whom you are sharing, chatting, and e-mailing, always.

## Facebooking on the Down Low

You have a lot of privacy options to choose from if you want to use Facebook and not give away too much of yourself to too many people. It is also possible to use Facebook to keep up with other people without actually having to share much yourself. This is called lurking. If you want to be able to lurk on Facebook without sharing too much of yourself, it's possible to set your account to the maximum privacy controls. The method of doing this changes frequently, but the capability is always there.

Simply go to your privacy settings and select from several options, including how you connect with people. Here, you can select who can see your profile, who can send you messages, who can send you friend requests, and who can look you up using your provided telephone number and e-mail address (which experts recommend you should avoid sharing). For each option, choose the most limited choice. If you select "Everyone," then your profile and its content will be public. If you select "Friends Only," then only people you have accepted as friends will be able to see your content.

Doing this means only people you have friended will be able to tell you are on Facebook. You can read other people's content but nobody can see you. This detracts from the interactive purpose of Facebook, but it does keep your information very private.

# CHAPTER TWO

# CONTROLLING WHO CAN SEE YOUR CONTENT

**A**lthough it's a good idea to skip sharing something on Facebook that has the potential to open yourself up to harm, Facebook is not an all-or-nothing program: you have some control over refining your audience every time you share something.

It's important to be aware of the various settings available on Facebook that allow you to customize who is able to see the content you publish on your timeline. In addition, you can make choices about how much content from a friend's timeline you are exposed to.

Privacy and other settings in Facebook change relatively frequently. It's possible that how you adjust these settings will be slightly different by the time you are reading this book. Use Facebook's help center or visit the privacy settings to learn the current steps for adjusting these settings.

You can opt to have a very accessible account that anyone can see or post content to, or you can make your account accessible only to people you are "friends" with.

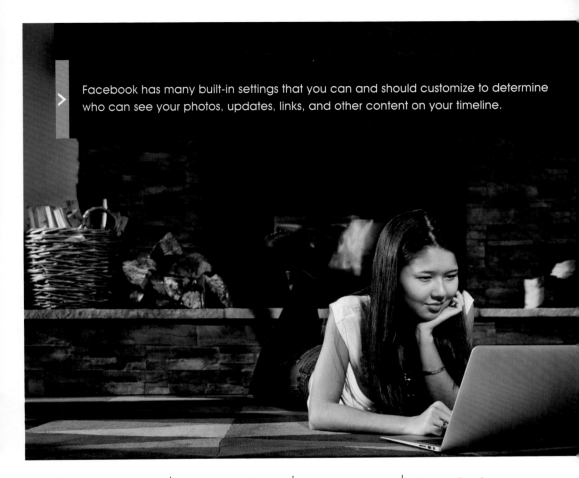

Facebook has many built-in settings that you can and should customize to determine who can see your photos, updates, links, and other content on your timeline.

But you can also customize who can see what content, including individual status updates. Facebook has made it even easier to decide who can see what by putting the controls right next to the related content on your timeline.

## Managing Who Sees What

Facebook makes it so all friends are not created equal. You can create categories of friends, such as "Family" or "Close Friends." Then you can select for specific content to be visible (or to be invisible) only to people in these

## > WHO'S WATCHING ME?

Anyone who uses Facebook has been, at least once, curious about whether a certain person has been checking out his or her profile. Maybe you wonder if the boy or girl you have a crush on is checking out what music you like or whether your mom is checking out what kinds of things you are posting in your status updates. Or maybe you are just curious about whether you are getting many visitors at all.

There are many fake applications circulating that claim they can show you who has been viewing your page. But here's the thing: there is no way to know who is looking at your timeline. These programs are spam and should be reported as such. These are potentially dangerous programs that attempt to get a user to give up his or her Facebook password and then release a virus to that user and his or her friends.

Facebook is very diligent about removing these scam applications, so you should report them. You can report something as spam in the menu that appears next to any status update on Facebook. If you cannot find this feature, search for "reporting spam" in Facebook's Help Center. If you think the person posting the spam was hacked, tell him or her to visit the "Security" section of the Help Center for help.

categories. If you post content that is relevant only to your baseball team, you can make a group called "Baseball" and share those posts only with team members.

When you post a status update on your timeline, there are other ways to choose who sees it. Next to the "Post" button on the bottom right of the status update box, there is another button that you can click to select who can see the specific status update. You can make it "Public" (anyone who can see your account can read your status update,

The privacy settings available on Facebook provide several options for protecting yourself online. Knowing what these settings are and mean can make your Facebook experience far safer.

even if you're not friends) or choose to show it only to "Friends," "Friends Except Acquaintances," or "Only Me."

You can click "Custom" to select individuals you want to make posts visible to or hidden from. This is a little more time consuming, as you may have to weed through hundreds of friends to select the few you want to include or exclude from a status update, video, or whatever you want to share. It's worth taking the time to create categories for your friends.

You can also control who sees the general parts of your profile, as opposed to status updates. For example, each user's timeline has an "About" section, where information about the person is listed. This includes hometown, birth date, occupation, education, and so on. There is a menu of choices for who can see this content. Choices range from "Everyone" to "Only Me," so you can be as open or private as you are comfortable with.

You can select to review tags other people want to put on your status updates or photos. A tag is a label—a person's name—that is attached to a photograph or status update. In your privacy settings, you can adjust the tagging options so that you will be asked to review and approve any tags others put on your content before they appear. You can also select to review tags of you that people want to put on their own posts and decide whether you want the tagged content to appear on your timeline.

If you aren't sure who can currently see content on your timeline, use the "View" tool to see what your profile looks

Sometimes other people post content that offends you, such as violent photos or even pornography. If you see something inappropriate, report it.

like to the public. This will allow you to see what your profile looks like to others. If you're not happy, take the time to make appropriate changes. You can look for help in changing your privacy settings by doing a general search on Facebook.

## Unfriending, Hiding, and Blocking

Everyone regrets friending someone on Facebook at some time. Perhaps it's a friend who constantly posts new status updates—every hour, letting the world know exactly what he is up to, whether it's interesting or not. Or perhaps you have someone who sends you daily invites to play a game or who posts links to articles you are not interested in or find offensive.

Facebook is a social phenomenon. It may have started as a way to connect online with people you already know well offline, but it's grown into its own social sphere with its own rules of etiquette. Just as you know you shouldn't take a phone call in a quiet movie theater, there are rules about how to behave on Facebook. Some of them are very clear—you can't post pornography, for example—but others are more subtle. If someone constantly posts messages about his or her religious or political beliefs, for example, people may tire of reading the posts.

Although Facebook makes it easy to remove someone from your friends list, it can be a hard thing to do from a social standpoint. People sometimes act differently online than off, being more vocal about issues or even being less kind to others than they would feel comfortable being in person. It can be awkward to unfriend someone you like in person or spend time with at school or on your sports team.

Facebook has several options that allow you to limit the access you have to specific people's Facebook follies. You can choose those friends who are closest to you to see their updates in your news feed. You can select to hide a person so that you never see his or her Facebook activities in your news feed, but you will still be "friends." You can even hide specific posts or request to see only important posts made by a particular person.

But some people really do cross the line and deserve to be cut from your online life. If you unfriend someone, you can still see his or her activity on mutual friends' timelines. So if you unfriend Betty because she has been posting hurtful lies about you, but Betty is "friends" with your friend Kate, you will still be able to see when Betty posts on Kate's timeline. If even that is too much information, you can

If you have Facebook friends that you'd like to see less of but don't necessarily want to unfriend, you can hide them instead, so they can't "see" you and you can't "see" them.

block Betty. This means you can't see her Facebook activity anywhere, and she won't be able to send you messages through Facebook. Check out Facebook's Help Center for more on blocking, unfriending, and limiting what you see of other people's activity.

## > RESEARCH: YOU CAN ONLY HAVE SO MANY FRIENDS

It can be very tempting to fall into the competitive spirit of "collecting" Facebook friends. If you're really smart, though, you will be very picky about whom you choose to friend. Just because someone rides the same school bus as you or goes to the same gym doesn't mean you have to open up your Facebook profile to him or her. And just because Facebook suggests you may know someone doesn't mean you have to friend that person, either.

You don't have to feel bad about keeping your friend list to a reasonable number. Recent research by evolutionary biologist Robin Dunbar proposes that our ability to manage social relationships is preset by our brain size and that the largest number of social relationships it is possible to meaningfully maintain (this includes romantic partners, friends, colleagues, and family) is 150. If you have more friends than that, according to Dunbar, it will make it impossible to know very much about them. So when it comes to relationships, choose quality over quantity.

# Calling It Quits

At some stage you may decide you just want to quit Facebook. Whether it's to buy back some of the time you inevitably waste reading the site when you should be studying or whether it's because you want to duck the scene for a while, deleting your profile is something you might consider.

It is possible to delete your profile in its entirety. You might want to do this if you've had some trouble with cyberbullying or if you've connected with too many people whom you don't want to unfriend (and face having to explain why). Or perhaps you've posted things you regret, and you just want to erase it all. There are lots of reasons to think about leaving Facebook. Before you do, though, you can request to download your content before it's deleted. See the Help Center to find out how to do this.

If quitting outright is too scary, perhaps you just need a little break. You can also deactivate your account, making it disappear from Facebook so nobody can find it. However, your profile will not be permanently deleted and can be reactivated in its entirety when you wish. Search for "deactivate my account" in the Help Center to learn how to do this.

# CHAPTER THREE

# FACEBOOK RESPONSIBILITY

**F**acebook is a tool that gives its users a wide audience for their content. Its uses extend beyond sharing photos of your new puppy with your cousin in California. Businesses use it to advertise to and connect with potential and existing customers. Organizations, be they political, like Democrats Abroad, or ones that target a particular group, such as Girl Scouts of America, have Facebook sites that are used to share relevant messages or encourage people to join a cause. Facebook is an incredibly effective tool for spreading your word—whatever it may be—far and wide.

But this does not mean that anything goes. Because it is such a powerful tool, Facebook has to have some standards in order to ensure that people use it for positive activity. It's also more than a tool: Facebook is a business. The business relies on people being willing to join the site and participate in social networking in order to make a profit and stay alive. If people do not feel safe using Facebook, they will not use it.

This chapter looks at some of the rules for using Facebook responsibly. That means using it without causing

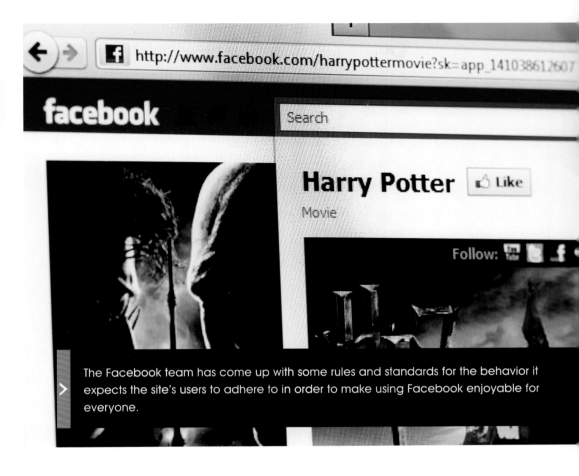

The Facebook team has come up with some rules and standards for the behavior it expects the site's users to adhere to in order to make using Facebook enjoyable for everyone.

any damage to anyone else or without putting yourself in danger.

## Reviewing Your Promise: The Statement of Rights and Responsibilities

When signing up for a Facebook account, there are certain agreements that Facebook asks you to comply with.

These are taken very seriously by Facebook, and violation of these agreements can result in the removal of a profile or group page.

The "Statement of Rights and Responsibilities" outlines the expectations Facebook has of its users, as well as what users can expect of Facebook. The first is privacy. Facebook keeps an updated "Data Use Policy" page on which it lets users know exactly what the site can do with the content your provide. Visit this often to be sure you are comfortable with current policy

Facebook asks you to commit to various rules regarding safety, security, and other people's rights. These include agreeing that you will not post spam or viruses knowingly on the site, and that you will not intentionally try to crash the site or post offensive material (see the next section for more on what is considered offensive).

Users must agree to register only as themselves, rather than assume another identity and create a false site. Users must be thirteen or older, cannot be convicted sex offenders, and cannot have more than one personal account.

There are many such agreements outlined in the "Statement of Rights and Responsibilities." It is worth reviewing the points to ensure that you do not violate any of them. Although these are not necessarily illegal actions, they are considered serious violations of Facebook policy. Engaging in them can lead to the permanent removal of your account.

# Understanding the Facebook Community Standards

In your hometown there are certain rules about what you can and cannot do. These rules are in place to ensure that everyone who lives in the town can enjoy a good life without anyone ruining things for anyone else. For example, your town may have laws about where dogs are allowed to wander off-leash or that determine at what time of day your neighbors have to stop blasting music on their balcony.

Like any community, Facebook is a nice place to be when people are respectful of each other and treat each other kindly. Facebook has established standards that determine what you can and cannot post. These standards aim to prevent users from being subjected to material that Facebook considers offensive, such as nudity and pornography. Because not everyone defines "offensive" the same way—something that is objectionable to one person may not be to someone else—Facebook reserves the right to delete any content that it determines is inappropriate. This has caused some controversy, as when the company removed photos showing a woman breastfeeding in 2012.

Facebook also does not allow content that is threatening, as in someone posting threats to another user or to a public figure, nor does it allow content that threatens or shows self-harm. In 2011, Facebook introduced a suicide prevention tool to provide help to users who post

# > FACEBOOK AND THE CLASSROOM

Technology is everywhere these days. Computers and telephone technology are essential to how we share and receive information. Facebook and social networking have become essential tools in the worlds of business, politics, and media. Technology, and Facebook in particular, can have an appropriate place in the classroom.

This doesn't mean you can waste time in biology class updating your status to share how boring class is. But your teacher may use Facebook to start a group for your class, updating members—which can include students and parents—on what assignments you are working on or to share photos from classroom activities.

Facebook can also help your class reach beyond the confines of the classroom to attend virtual lectures, check out museums that you can't visit in person, do research, follow a political issue, or play educational video games through the site. There are many educational, informative, positive uses for Facebook that can make it an invaluable tool for learning in the classroom. If you have ideas about how you can use the site to extend learning opportunities in your school, talk with your principal and teachers about it. Remember to always apply the same rules of privacy and responsible community behavior to any classroom or group site that you would to your own personal timeline.

any content indicating suicidal thoughts. Friends can report such content by clicking a report option next to any post on the site and choosing "violence or harmful behavior."

Other types of content that can lead to harm and are therefore not allowed are graphic violence, hate speech, bullying, and harassment. All of these can be reported by clicking the appropriate option in the menu next to the post. You can indicate whether the post is harassing you or a friend, or you can report it as spam, hate speech, sexually explicit, violent or harmful, or as suspicion that a friend's account has been hacked. If you cannot find the menu to access the reporting options, check the Help Center.

## Reporting Abuse: What Can I Expect?

Facebook's criteria for removing a post, timeline (personal profile), or group is outlined on its Community Standards page. Content that violates these terms will be removed, and depending on the circumstances, legal action can be taken against the offender.

However, reporting abuse does not guarantee that the post, profile, or group in question will be removed. Facebook makes the decision about what content is appropriate or inappropriate to share on the site. This is because not everything that irritates or angers a person is actually offensive. Just because you disagree with something doesn't make it abusive.

For example, perhaps you have a friend who feels strongly about a politician and you don't agree with his or her point of view. If reading the comments about this politician angers you, that is not enough basis for having it removed. Instead, look into blocking the person or unsubscribing from him or her, or just let the person know you find the material offensive and may have to remove him or her as a friend.

Facebook is a diverse community that provides a platform for people of many different mindsets around the world to share their ideas. Protecting individuals and groups from

Although you can't report a friend for posting annoying political views that differ from yours, some content is absolutely banned from Facebook and should be reported.

offensive content while at the same time protecting free speech can be really difficult. Facebook has had to make some controversial decisions to let content remain on the site in the name of free speech.

In the past this has included a page that encouraged users to burn the Israeli flag and other pages that celebrate murderers and political tyrants. Facebook remains neutral and therefore has to allow groups that voice strong opinions about controversial topics, such as gay rights and abortion, even though these groups may offend some users.

# Minors on Facebook

One of the big concerns that parents and community members have is that Facebook exposes children to too many risks. Children and young adults can be less cautious than more mature users when it comes to sharing content and private information on the site. This can expose young people to stalkers, sexual predators, or bullies. Because of these risks, Facebook does not allow children under the age of thirteen to join and encourages parents and guardians to monitor the Facebook activities of all minors.

Facebook has a safety center that provides advice for parents, teachers, and teens about how to help minors use Facebook safely. It encourages parents and teachers to learn the language of Facebook so that they know what it means to "poke" someone, what the timeline is, and what it means to "friend" or "unfriend." To users of Facebook, this language is second nature, but adults who do not use the site should be clued in to what all these terms mean.

## Helping Parents Feel Comfortable with Facebook

Teens will be happy to know that Facebook doesn't just try to get parents and teachers to interfere with your good time online. In fact, it encourages parents to allow children to have their privacy online, to a certain degree. The safety center states that parents should apply the same boundaries online as they would off-line. It makes an analogy between going on Facebook and going to a friend's house: if parents trust you enough to visit without harming yourself or others, then they should respect your growing independence and need for privacy—while, of course, balancing this with ensuring your safety.

Here are some other Facebook tips for parents. Perhaps you can suggest some of these to your parents if they are feeling uncomfortable about you using Facebook. The more parents understand about the site and the more teens show that they are aware of the risks and are actively protecting themselves and their online privacy, the more comfortable parents may become with minors on the site.

- If you don't understand the technology, ask your children to explain it to you.

Talking with your parents about Facebook and what kinds of content you share and what role the site plays in your friendships can help calm fears they may have about the dangers of social networking.

- If you're not already on Facebook, consider joining. That way you'll understand what it's all about.
- Create a Facebook group for your family so you will have a private space to share photos and keep in touch.
- Talk about and be sure you understand the online safety basics. Talk about technology safety just like you talk about safety while driving and playing sports.

# 10 GREAT QUESTIONS

## TO ASK A SOCIAL NETWORKING EXPERT

**1** When did you get started using social media? How did you learn how?

**2** What first attracted you to the idea of social networking?

**3** How has social media changed the way people connect?

**4** What is the greatest benefit of social media?

**5** What are some negative consequences of using social media?

**6** What is your favorite social networking site?

**7** What do you most use social media for (work, friendship)?

**8** How much time per day do you spend on social networking sites?

**9** How do you build an audience on your blog, Twitter, or Facebook?

**10** What makes someone a social media expert?

# CHAPTER FOUR

# ALL ABOUT SECURITY

There are many actions you can take to have a safe, hassle-free Facebook experience. The best way to guard your privacy is not to share anything unless you would want the whole world to see or read it. Barring that, you have a lot of options for customizing who can access content on your Facebook profile.

However, none of these options are in your control if someone hacks your account. If your account is hacked, it means that someone has managed to get access to your account and can control the settings and content. With access to your account, a hacker can distribute computer viruses so it looks as though they came from you.

Facebook security is about more than protecting your content. It's about protecting users everywhere from malicious software, meaning files that do damage. Facebook takes security very seriously and has recently joined with five different computer security firms to protect Facebook's content. These companies will monitor links that are posted on Facebook to look for viruses. But security is everyone's responsibility. This chapter looks at how you can protect

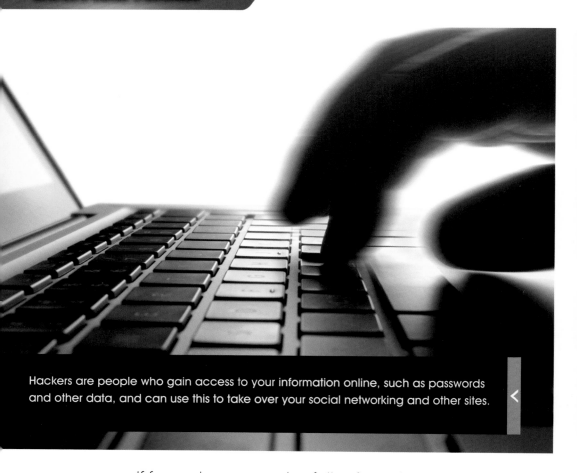

Hackers are people who gain access to your information online, such as passwords and other data, and can use this to take over your social networking and other sites.

yourself from other potential pitfalls of Facebook, like online fraud and hacking.

## Password Protection

A lot of actions that lead to a more secure Facebook experience are common sense. The first step to keeping your profile secure is choosing a strong, effective password. Avoid obvious passwords like your pet's name, your birthday, or the name of your school.

In the last year or so, user profiles of two major social networking sites—Gawker and LinkedIn—were hacked. The most common passwords used for both sites were passwords of consecutive numbers. For example, two of the top ten passwords for LinkedIn members were 1234 and 12345, while three passwords in the Gawker top ten were 12345, 123456, and 12345678. These passwords were of course easy for the users to remember, but they were just as easy for a hacker to guess.

Other weak passwords are those that contain only lowercase letters and spell out a common word. Potential hackers can attempt what is called a "dictionary attack," using your username with common dictionary words like "love" until they find a match. Mixing in some capital letters, such as "LoVe" makes your password a little stronger, but it's still pretty weak.

The strongest passwords mix in numbers and what are called special characters, such as an ampersand (&) or asterisk (*). So for example, "1LoVe!" is a far stronger password than simply "love."

Once you have a strong password, always keep it to yourself. You wouldn't give someone the key to your diary or the code for unlocking your sim card on your phone (at least you shouldn't!), so don't be loose with your password. The more people who know it, the more you put yourself and your profile at risk. It is also a good idea to change your password from time to time.

This may seem obvious, but it is very important to keep in mind: when you are using a public computer, at school or in an Internet café, always be sure to log out before you step away from the machine. If you remain logged in, the next person to come along will have full access to your account. To log out, click the downward facing arrow at the top right of your screen and select "Log Out" from the drop-down menu that appears.

You should also clear the cache and delete any cookies from a public computer after a Facebook session. The steps for doing this vary depending on your browser. To learn how to clear the cache and delete cookies on your browser, search Google for the steps. It's quick and easy to do.

## Check Your Security Settings

Facebook allows you to opt in and out of various levels of security settings, but you have to be aware of your options. Also be aware that these settings change from time to time. It's important to review the current options every now and then, and make sure you understand them. You can change security options by going to the account settings or by doing a search on the Facebook Help Center.

You will see several options that help ensure you know who is accessing your account and when. For example, you can select to have Facebook notify you by text or e-mail every time your account is accessed from a mobile device you haven't used before. You can also choose to have

## > SECURITY TIPS FOR MINORS

Young people who use Facebook can unfortunately fall victim to predators who are not whom they claim to be. It's a sad reality, but teens on Facebook need to be especially cautious when securing their Facebook profiles.

Facebook takes certain steps to protect minors who use the site. You must be at least thirteen to have a Facebook account, and Facebook has some special security settings aimed at teens—including an option to prevent a teen's profile from showing up in public searches.

a special password required every time you access your account from an unrecognized computer or mobile device.

You can also review current and recent active sessions—meaning times when your account has been accessed by a user. This tells you where your account was accessed from (geographic location), on what date, and on what kind of device. If you see any sessions on unfamiliar devices or in places in the world where you were not, you can disable that activity to end the session.

## Beware of Phishing Schemes

"Phishing" is a term for a kind of online fraud in which people try to access your password information in order to hijack your site. With a phishing scam, an e-mail that appears to be from a legitimate source, such as a bank or site like PayPal, tries to get you to reveal your password or other personal details, usually with a threat to your account if you don't respond right away.

This sense of urgency makes people react without thinking. If you take the time to read such an e-mail carefully, it is easy to detect a phishing scam. Sometimes the logo

close and trusted colleagues need your assistance in the transfer of ...

This fund was generated from over-invoicing of contracts executed by the PTF ... were discovered while we were reviewing the PTF accounts.

From our discoveries, these contracts have been executed and the contractor ... the over-invoiced amount is the funds, we want your corporate entity to help us receive.

What we want from you is a good and reliable company or personal Account ...

Details should include the following:

1. Name of Bank
2. Address of Bank with Fax & Tel. No.
3. Account Number
4. Beneficiary/Signatory to Account (Account Name)

Upon the Successful crediting of your Account, The fund will be shared as follows:
1. 20% for you and your assistance
2. 75% for myself & my Colleagues
3. 5% for contingency expenses

Please after your first reply through e-mail. I will want us to continue further ... that your involvement ... into it.

Phishing scams are tricks people use to try and get others to reveal their private information, such as passwords and account numbers. Never reveal this content without being positive it's for a legitimate reason.

when repl... can reac... ...phone nu...

doesn't look quite like the actual logo of the company the e-mail is pretending to be from, or the link you're being asked to click doesn't include the usual Web site name of the company.

If the e-mail is unprofessional—full of grammar and spelling mistakes and perhaps even misspelling your name—then it is probably a scam. If you are unsure if something is a scam, contact the bank or company that the message is supposedly from and have someone there confirm that the e-mail is legitimate.

# What To Do if Your Account Is Hacked

Unfortunately many hackers are as intelligent and motivated as the people who develop security systems for sites like Facebook and other places online. There is no guarantee that you will not be hacked at some point. The best you can do is make it as hard as possible for someone to have full access to your passwords and profile.

If you start to notice strange messages being sent from your account, you have been hacked. For example, if posts are appearing on your friends' timelines that are seemingly from you but that you did not post yourself, your account has been hacked. Often these posts read something like, "OMG you will not believe how much weight I lost this month!" with a link to a diet pill ad or will show a link to a video proclaiming that it shows something incredible that you just had to share with your friends.

If you have indeed been hacked, first alert your friends not to open any links they receive from you. Then, fix the problem by going to the Help Center. There is an option that will tell you what to do if you are hacked. Facebook will first have you reset your password and will let you know whether your new password is weak or strong. Then, you will have the opportunity to undo anything the hacker has changed or posted through your account. During this time, your account will be locked, so only you can access it. When you have undone all the hacker's dirty work, your account will be unlocked.

If you use the same account for your e-mail or any other account, be sure you change your passwords for these as well. It's a good idea to always use different passwords for different password-protected sites you visit online. This prevents a hacker from having access to everything as soon as he or she has the password for one account.

Make sure you report any suspicious posts to Facebook, and pay attention to what activity is seemingly coming from your account. If you see suspicious messages or posts from friends, let them know about it so they can protect their accounts from hackers, too.

# ACCESSING APPLICATIONS, GAMES, AND WEB SITES WITH FACEBOOK

# CHAPTER FIVE

**A**pplications are little extras that can make interacting with people on Facebook more fun. They provide entertainment, such as the very popular games Words With Friends and CityVille, and also provide more focused functionality, such as Pinterest, for sharing everything that a person likes.

Some applications come automatically with your Facebook account, such as Notes, and have been created by Facebook itself. These are trustworthy, as are many others created by third-party developers. Some of these applications, however, developed by people who are not part of Facebook, may be spam or can spread viruses.

Anybody can create an application for Facebook. There is not a testing or verification process, as there is with Apple iPhone applications. Before downloading an application, you should try to find out more about it, such as who developed it, how many people are using it, what

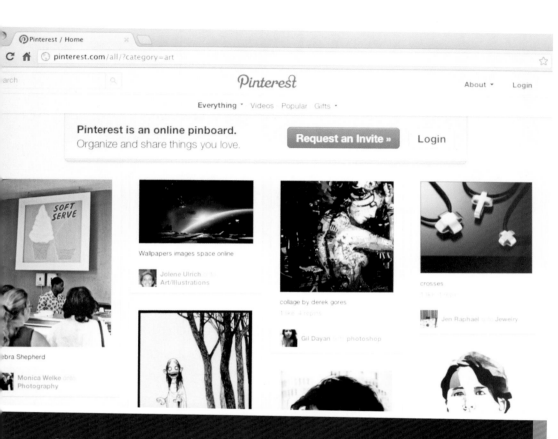

Pinterest is a site for sharing common interests with other people. Pinterest users can use the Pinterest Facebook app in order to share their finds via Facebook.

users say about it, and how much of your personal data the application can access.

Some applications are perfectly wonderful and make the Facebook experience better, but others can cause serious irritation to you and others. Let's look at how to tell the good from the bad applications, how to protect your privacy, and how not to annoy and be annoyed by others when it comes to sending application requests.

# Protecting Your Personal Data from Applications

Not everyone knows that their personal data—name, birth date, and so on—can be accessed by applications that their friends use. This means that even if you do not personally use an application, it can still find out information about you.

If you have concerns about keeping your privacy online, and everybody should, this will not be a comfortable thought. The most foolproof way to protect yourself from having unwanted applications access your personal data is to disallow any applications, period. You can change this where you access your privacy settings.

But that is an extreme action that you may not want to take. Applications are, after all, part of the fun of using Facebook, and many of them are harmless, useful, and enjoyable. As an alternative to blocking all applications, you can adjust the setting for how other people use your content. You can change this in your privacy settings as well.

# Applications: Another Way to Overshare

You should be wary of applications that will do things like send you constant notifications or cover your wall in frequent and repetitive updates. For example, some games will automatically post on your wall when you've taken your turn, and you may not always want everyone to know you are playing a game when you should be studying.

And frankly, not everyone really wants to know what you are doing at all times of the day. When the music application Spotify posted each song every user was listening to on their wall, there was an outcry of "I don't care what you're listening to" from many Facebook users—not to mention that some people don't want everyone to know

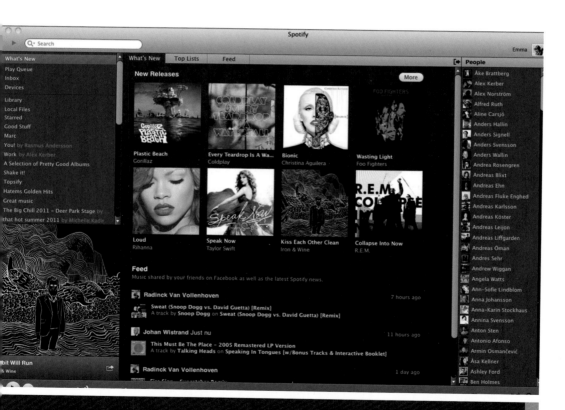

The Spotify music app is popular on Facebook. But not all apps are from reputable sources. Always check out apps before recommending them to friends, or you may just be spreading spam.

they are blasting their secret pleasure in what they think is the privacy of their own home. Make sure you know what you are permitting an application to do when you agree to use it.

# Authorizing/Deauthorizing Applications

When you authorize an application, you are opening up your profile to it, just as when you friend someone. When you first click on an application, before you can use it, you should see a dialog box asking you for permission to access your basic information, like your friends list, and also your "likes." In some cases, an application will ask to access your contact information. Be absolutely sure you know what you are allowing before you agree.

If you want to review or change the settings attached to a particular application, you can check them where you access your account settings. You will see a list of all the applications you are currently using. You can adjust who will see posts made on your behalf by the application as well as when the application will notify you. If you want to deactivate or delete an application, follow the same steps for editing settings and remove the application.

You also have an option to turn off the ability for Facebook to share information about applications you use off-line, as mentioned earlier in this chapter. However, that takes away some of the pleasure of using apps. Not all

## > REMEMBER NOT ALL APPS ARE BAD

Although there are some definite negative aspects to applications, try not to think of them as the enemy. If you get several requests that annoy you, you can just choose to decline or ignore them. But although you should always exercise caution when allowing any program access to your data, not all applications are bad things with sinister motives.

Some applications can be educational and fun, and you should be open to using these as part of your interactive Facebook experience. Google articles that review applications before using them, or talk to your friends about what apps they find most useful. Follow basic security measures, and be picky, but explore and take advantage of the creative and inventive applications that people have developed for you to enjoy.

applications are bad things, and with some applications sharing information with friends is part of the fun of using the app.

For example, if you run with your iPhone using Nike Plus, the application will automatically post on Facebook the distance you completed when you finish your exercise. Sharing this information can give you more incentive to go farther. It is also a good way to keep up with other friends with whom you may be training.

# Avoid Spamming and Being Spammed

Recently, a status update along the lines of "This person does not want any invitations to FarmVille" became very popular. FarmVille was a very popular app when it first came out, but many people soon tired of friends' requests to join the game. Rather than block a friend who sends you frequent annoying requests, you can choose to block all requests from the particular game.

Game requests in particular can be very frustrating to receive each day. Sending too many game requests is a good way to get blocked.

Similarly, your friends will appreciate not being spammed. When you use an application, you are often asked to share it with twelve of your friends before your activity in the application is shared on your timeline. Opt out of this unless you know your friends will be interested.

Some friends will be interested in playing games and knowing what workout you completed in a particular day. In order to keep such friends informed while not annoying everyone else with updates they don't want, you can select to share application-related updates with a particular group of friends.

Facebook is a great tool for keeping in touch with friends and family and making new contacts. While it has its benefits, there are also many reasons to be cautious while using it. If you can take the proper precautions, using Facebook can be a rewarding and fun experience.

# MYTHS AND FACTS

**Myth:** Facebook is going to start charging members for using the site.

**Fact:** This rumor has been around since the beginning of Facebook, and it's completely untrue. Facebook has no plans to charge users for signing up with the site.

**Myth:** Facebook sells your information to advertisers.

**Fact:** Facebook does not share your personal information with anyone. The Help Center is very clear on this point: "We do not share your personal information with people or services you don't want. We do not give advertisers access to your personal information. We do not and never will sell any of your information to anyone."

**Myth:** People can tell if I've viewed their profiles.

**Fact:** There is currently no application that can let you know who views your profile. Programs that claim to do so are spam and should be reported.

# GLOSSARY

**applications** Small programs, such as games, that you can use with Facebook.

**block** When you block someone on Facebook, that person can no longer see your profile, send you messages, or add you as a friend.

**cover photo** On your timeline, your cover photo appears across the top of your page.

**event** This feature allows you to invite a group of people to a gathering, such as a meeting or a party.

**friend** When you connect with people on Facebook, you "friend" them.

**groups** A way to organize groups of friends with whom you share an interest, such as members of your soccer team or book club.

**like** Giving positive feedback to a status update, photo, or comments by clicking "Like."

**lists** You can organize your friends into categories, or lists.

**news feed** A list of status updates and other posts from your friends that appears on your timeline. It is constantly updated.

**notes** An application that allows users to write longer status updates or share ideas in more detail.

**page** A profile for a business or organization on Facebook.

**password**  A series of letters, numbers, and special characters that you create to protect anyone from accessing your account.

**phishing**  A way for scammers to try to trick you into giving up personal information, like your Facebook password.

**profile**  Your page on Facebook where all of your content appears.

**timeline**  The latest design of a Facebook profile page, which was previously called a wall; it organizes all of your content chronologically.

**social media**  Interactive web- and mobile-phone-technologies that allow people to share comments and opinions.

**spam**  Electronic junk mail. Spam should be reported.

**status update**  A short message you write on Facebook that appears on your profile and in your friends' news feeds.

**wall**  The original name for your profile page, where you and friends can post photos, links, or messages that all your friends can see.

Canadian Centre for Child Protection, Inc.
615 Academy Road
Winnipeg, MB R3N 0E7
Canada
(204) 945-5735
Web site: https://protectchildren.ca
This charitable organization is dedicated to the personal
safety of all children and to reducing child victimization by
providing programs and services to the Canadian public.

Common Sense Media
650 Townsend, Suite 435
San Francisco, CA 94103
(415) 863-0600
Web site: http://www.commonsensemedia.org
Common Sense Media is dedicated to improving the lives
of kids and families by providing trustworthy information
and education to help them thrive in a world of media
and technology.

CyberAngels Internet Safety Education Program
982 East 89th Street
Brooklyn, NY 11236
Web site: http://www.cyberangels.org
CyberAngels is one of the oldest and most respected
online safety education programs in the world.

Family Online Safety Institute
400 7th Street NW, Suite 306
Washington, DC 20004
Web site: http://www.fosi.org
This international, nonprofit membership organization
   works to develop a safer Internet by identifying and
   promoting best practices, tools, and methods that also
   respect free speech.

Office of the Privacy Commissioner of Canada
112 Kent Street
Place de Ville Tower B, Third Floor
Ottawa, ON K1A 1H3
Canada
(800) 282-1376
Web site: http://www.priv.gc.ca
The Office of the Privacy Commissioner of Canada provides
   information and resources to help people understand
   their personal information rights and obligations under
   Canada's two privacy laws, the Personal Information
   Protection and Electronic Documents Act (PIPEDA) and
   the Privacy Act.

Web Wise Kids
P.O. Box 27203
Santa Ana, CA 92799

Web site: http://www.webwisekids.org
Web Wise Kids provides unique and effective resources to equip young people to safely use and enjoy the latest digital technologies.

## Web Sites

Due to the changing nature of Internet links, Rosen Publishing has developed an online list of Web sites related to the subject of this book. This site is updated regularly. Please use this link to access the list:

http://www.rosenlinks.com/21C/FBSP

Abram, Carolyn. *Facebook for Dummies*. Hoboken, NJ: Wiley, 2012.

Beaver, Kevin. *Hacking for Dummies*. Hoboken, NJ: Wiley, 2010.

Belicove, Mika E. *The Complete Idiot's Guide to Facebook*. New York, NY: Alpha, 2011.

Claypoole, Ted, et. al. *Protecting Your Internet Identity: Are You Naked Online?* Lanham, MD: Rowman & Littlefield, 2012.

Dhanjani, Nitesh. *Hacking: The Next Generation*. Sebastopol, CA: O'Reilly Media, 2009.

Essany, Michael. *Mark Zuckerberg: Ten Lessons in Leadership*. Memphis, TN: New Beginnings, 2012.

Gunter, Sherry Kinkoph. *Sams Teach Yourself Facebook in 10 Minutes*. Indianapolis, IN: Sams, 2010.

Greenburg, Grant. *Facebook and Privacy: What You Need to Know to Keep Your Privacy Safe*. Seattle, WA: Amazon Digital Services, 2010.

Grossman, Lev. *The Connector: How Facebook's Mark Zuckerberg Rewired Our World and Changed the Way We Live*. New York, NY: Time, 2010.

Hunter, Nick. *Cyber Bullying*. Mankato, MN: Heinemann-Raintree, 2011.

Ivester, Matt. *LOL...OMG! What Every Student Needs to Know About Online Reputation Management, Digital*

*Citizenship, and Cyberbullying*. Seattle, WA: CreateSpace, 2011.

Jacobs, Thomas. *Teen Cyberbullying Investigated*. Minneapolis, MN: Free Spirit Publishing, 2010.

Kerpen, Dave. *Likeable Social Media: How to Delight Your Customers, Create an Irresistible Brand, and Be Generally Amazing on Facebook (And Other Social Networks)*. New York, NY: McGraw-Hill, 2011.

Kirkpatrick, David. *The Facebook Effect: The Inside Story of the Company That Is Connecting the World*. New York, NY: Simon & Schuster, 2011.

Martin, Gail. *30 Days to Social Media Success: The 30 Day Results Guide to Making the Most of Twitter, Blogging, LinkedIN, and Facebook*. Pompton Plains, NJ: Career Press, 2010.

Mezrich, Ben. *The Accidental Billionaires: The Founding of Facebook: A Tale of Sex, Money, Genius, and Betrayal*. Garden City, NY: Anchor Books, 2010.

O'Reilly, Tim, and Sarah Milstein. *The Twitter Book*. Sebastopol, CA: O'Reilly Media, 2011.

Vanderveer, E. A. *Facebook: The Missing Manual*. Cambridge, MA: Pogue Press, 2011.

Awl, Dave. *Facebook Me!* Berkeley, CA: Peachpit Press, 2010.

Collier, Anne, and Larry Magid. *A Parent's Guide to Facebook.* ConnectSafely.org and iKeepSafe Coalition, 2012. Retrieved August 1, 2012 (http://www.connectsafely.org/pdfs/fbparents.pdf).

Constine, Josh. "App Discovery by Quality, Not Popularity." Techcrunch.com, May 9, 2012. Retrieved July 18, 2012 (http://techcrunch.com/2012/05/09/facebook-app-center).

Differencesmag. "Youth and Social Media." SocialMediaWeek.org, February 15, 2012. Retrieved July 2, 2012 (http://socialmediaweek.org/newyork/2012/02/15/youth-and-social-media).

Facebook. "Facebook Data Use Policy." Facebook.com. Retrieved July 20, 2012 (https://www.facebook.com/about/privacy).

Facebook. "Facebook Safety Center." Facebook.com. Retrieved July 15, 2012 (https://www.facebook.com/safety).

Facecrooks. "How to Lockdown Your Facebook Account for Maximum Privacy and Security." Facecrooks.com, April 16, 2012. Retrieved July 29, 2012 (http://facecrooks.com/Internet-Safety-Privacy/how-to-lockdown-your-facebook-account-for-maximum-privacy-and-security.html).

Hartley-Parkinson, Richard. "You Can't Hug a Facebook Friend." *Daily Mail*, August 15, 2011. Retrieved July 29, 2012 (http://www.dailymail.co.uk/sciencetech /article-2026086/Facebook-Young-people-spend -time-online-theyre-lonely-elderly.html).

Lenhart, Amanda, et. al. "Teens, Kindness and Cruelty on Social Network Sites." Pew Internet, November 9, 2011. Retrieved July 20, 2012 (http://pewinternet. org/Reports/2011/Teens-and-social-media.aspx).

McCarthy, Linda, et. al. "A Guide to Facebook Security." Facebook.com, 2012. Retrieved July 30, 2012 (https://www.facebook.com/safety/attachment /Guide%20to%20Facebook%20Security.pdf).

Mitrano, Tracy. "A Wider World: Youth, Privacy, and Social Networking Technologies." Educause Review Online, January 1, 2006. Retrieved July 28, 2012 (http://www.educause.edu/ero/article/wider-world -youth-privacy-and-social-networking-technologies).

Natarajan, Ramesh. "The Ultimate Guide for Creating Strong Passwords." TheGeekStuff.com, June 8, 2008. Retrieved July 22, 2012 (http://www.thegeekstuff .com/2008/06/the-ultimate-guide-for-creating-strong -passwords).

Rasmussen, Rune. "Official Guide to Facebook Secruity." KidsandMedia.co.uk, August 29, 2011. Retrieved

July 29, 2012 (http://www.kidsandmedia.co.uk
/official-guide-to-facebook-security).

Sameer, Misna. "Impact of Social Networking Sites on
Youth." YouthKiAwaaz.com, June 2, 2011. Retrieved
August 1, 2012 (http://www.youthkiawaaz.com
/2011/06/social-networking-impact-youth).

Smith, Catharine. "Facebook Scams You Need to Know
About." *Huffington Post*, July 22, 2011. Retrieved August
1, 2012 (http://www.huffingtonpost.com/2011/05
/22/facebook-scams-hacks-attacks_n_864906.html).

Smith, Catharine. "The 15 Most Popular Facebook Apps
Ranked by AppData." *Huffington Post*, May 25, 2011.
Retrieved July 17, 2012 (http://www.huffingtonpost
.com/2010/11/22/15-most-popular-facebook
-apps_n_784978.html#s179561&title=15__Pet).

Suehle, Ruth. "Was Your LinkedIn Password Leaked?"
Wired.com, June 6, 2012. Retrieved July 2, 2012
(http://www.wired.com/geekmom/2012/06
/linkedin-data-breach).

*New York Times*. "Time Topics: Mark Zuckerberg." May 21,
2012. Retrieved July 3, 2012 (http://topics.nytimes.
com/topics/reference/timestopics/people/z/mark_e
_zuckerberg/index.html).

# INDEX

# About the Author

Tracy Brown studied journalism at Emerson College and the European Institute for International Communication and has written several books for young adults on a variety of topics. She lives in the Netherlands.

# Photo Credits

Cover (figure) Edyta Pawlowska/Shutterstock.com; cover (background) Annette Shaff/Shutterstock.com; pp. 4–5 © AP Images; p. 7 Justin Sullivan/Getty Images; p. 8 © iStockphoto.com/Sarun Laowong; p. 12 Peter Cade/Iconica/Getty Images; p. 15 Ron Levine/Lifesize/Getty Images; p. 17 © iStockphoto.com/Sam Burt Photography; p. 19 Blend Images/Hill Street Studios/the Agency Collection/Getty Images; p. 21 lev dolgachov/Shutterstock.com; p. 25 © iStockphoto.com/ilbusca; p. 30 Elie Bernager/ONOKY/Getty Images; p. 33 Robert Daly/OJO Images/Getty Images; p. 36 Mikael Damkier/Shutterstock.com; p. 40 Just One Film/Stockbyte/Getty Images; p. 44 © iStockphoto.com/Alberto Bogo; p. 46 Handout/MCT/Newscom; p. 49 Bloomberg/Getty Images.

Designer: Mike Moy; Editor: Bethany Bryan; Photo Researcher: Karen Huang